# Poems by an Aussie battler

**RON DAVIS**

SEAVIEW
PRESS

© Ron Davis 1997

This book is copyright. Apart from fair dealing as permitted under the *Copyright Act*, no part may be photocopied or in any way reproduced by any process without written permission. Please make inquiries to Seaview Press.

Illustrations by John Tolcher

Seaview Press
PO Box 234
Henley Beach
South Australia 5022
Ph: (08) 8235 1535: Fax (08) 8235 9144
e-mail: seaview@seaviewpress.com.au
http://www.seaviewpress.com.au

Seaview Press is a division of A.C.N. 075 827 851 Pty Ltd.


Printed in Australia by Copy Master
234 Currie Street
Adelaide
South Australia 5000


ISBN 1 876070 50 1

# Acknowledgments

To:
My critic, helper and editor, my lovely wife June.
My very good friends, the Smith family, Mary, Jim in
Coventry, and Pam in Surrey, England.
The three best mates a bloke could wish for,
Jacalynn Melville, Tracey Doherty, Colleen Walker.
It's with your help and encouragement that I
produced the book I promised you.

And to John Tolcher for his cartoons.

# About the author

Ron Davis was born in Victoria and raised in a mountainous area of Gippsland. He served four years in the Australian Navy during World War II, then for several years went walkabout, working on cattle stations in the outback of the Northern Territory. He came to Queensland when open-cut coal mining started in the central Queensland area and worked the mines before migrating to permanently live, then retire, on Magnetic Island, where he and his wife still reside at beautiful Horseshoe Bay.

# Contents

# The Aussie battlers

We came out from old Blighty
In the hold of a convict barque
Then they tossed us off in Botany Bay
Where conditions were real stark.

They left us all in leg irons
They left the chains around our necks
Then flogged us into building roads
And did their best to make us wrecks.

The years passed by the gang boss said,
'Here at last you have your pardon,
So take this axe and build a shack
Then start to make a garden.'

He married a homely little lass
And a family they did raise
Two sons in all they were their pride
And twenty cattle on the graze.

The old chap went a few years back
His sons they both branched out
We are the offspring of those folk
And now Australians, there's no doubt.

Our lives remained quite peaceful
Until the British gave a call,
'We need you in South Africa,
Where we have our backs against the wall.'

We were an untried fighter
But soon became a mighty force
When we saddled up our brumbies
To become the Aussie First Light Horse.

We left our wives and kids at home
To keep working on the farm
And hoped that in our absence
They wouldn't come to any harm.

We thought we won't be here that long
Before we even up the score
But a full three years did pass us by
Before we won this bloody war.

Now our kiddies they have all grown up
And have families of their own
But our peace is being shattered
It's time to take up arms again.

We foot-slogged from the trenches
Across the blood soaked Flanders dells
Then went to face up to the Turks
At the dreaded Dardanelles.

We fought them at Gallipoli
And at the Battle of the Somme
In fact there wasn't any place
Where we didn't tag along.

The Kaiser said, 'I've had enough,'
And conceded we had won
So now we are back on Aussie soil
Where our lives had first begun.

Then just another few short years
Another madman on the loose
By the name of Adolf Hitler
We have to go and cook his goose.

A full five years we battled on
Through desert, sand and sea
Up in the air we held our own
And where no Aussie ought to be.

They took us from all walks of life
We wore our battle dress with pride
We were a bit rough round the edges
But we took all in our stride.

Thinking back through all those years
And what we have achieved
Three full-scale wars have come and gone
And many times we were bereaved.

We battled fire and drought and flood
We survived the great Depression
We worked this land to make us great
But it's been a costly lesson.

Now the family tree has spread right out
We are no more in a cluster
So we're gathering at the old log shack
There to have a family muster.

I think I will have to go by coach
Though would rather jump the rattlers
To hear about my long-gone kin
The original AUSSIE BATTLERS.

# The Alice Springs Cup

They are coming in from north to south
From the west right to the east
And converging on the centre
For this test of man and beast.

This land is hot and dusty
It's no fit place for a palace
Where we hold this Aussie marathon
In a town they call the Alice.

There's some that come by horse float
There's some that come by plane
There's some that have to canter in
And there's some that come by train.

Down to Earth the colt from Perth
Has come across the Nullarbor
There's Blind as a Bat from Ballarat
And Spring Heeled Jack from Mangalore.

Salt Bush Bill from Broken Hill
Has come to toe the line
While Peg Leg Pete from up the street
Has arrived from Narromine.

Battling Bob from Yorkeys Knob
Has come across the plain
While Winnie the Pooh from outer Barcoo
Has just arrived by train.

The Old Black Crow is here from the south
He's been trained at Port Augusta
While the Grey Galah from Coolibah
Has finished the cattle muster.

Late for Work arrived from Bourke
To give this race a try
And the Tucker Box has just flown in
From the town of Gundagai.

Full of Gin is the local nag
Pulls the bread cart to and fro
She does this seven days a week
So is always on the go.

HE HE HE ... THIS'LL BE A ONE HORSE RACE.

Now they lined up all the jockeys
Said, 'This is a most important race,
Be sure to keep each bronco moving
And don't slacken up the pace.

'So grab your whips and saddles
Then get up on the scales
And when you get out on the track
Don't go running off the rails.'

The starter said, 'Right, on your marks
Then I'll send you on your way
So best of luck to one and all
Who have entered here this day.'

They took off in a cloud of dust
Went past the old windmill
Then slowed down to a steady walk
As they climbed up Miners' Hill.

They galloped past the water tank
They fairly shook the ground
As the bookie took off on his bike
To turn the halfway sign around.

The crowd was getting restless
There wasn't a horse in sight
So we all checked on the blankets
In case we had to spend the night.

The copper said, 'Now just keep calm
Here I'll keep law and order,'
As the Flying Doctor radioed in,
'They've just crossed the Queensland border.'

Then over the distant horizon
Came the local Full of Gin
Accompanied by the bookie
And on his face a big wide grin.

She cantered past the winning post
But there was very little cheer
As the punters drowned their sorrows
At the boozer full of beer.

The bookie he fast disappeared
He took off like a rocket
With all the punters' money
In his bottomless hip pocket.

The crowd just sat and wondered
How the bookie sold them up
And how Full of Gin, a cart horse
Managed to win the Alice Cup.

# At the gym

I helped a lady cross the street
Had done my boy Scout's deed
When two girls upon the footpath
Said, 'Who is that skinny weed?'

So I beat it down to Old Joe's Gym
I said, 'Tell me what you see,
And while you're thinking what to say,
Can you make a man of me?'

He walked around me once or twice
Said, 'There's some things that astound
With pinched-in gut and skinny legs
You're looking like a greyhound.

'Go over there and lift those weights
They're fifteen pounds, no more
And don't drop them on your dainty toes
I don't want to dent the floor.

'It will take two years of real hard work
Before you reach the stars
So break into a gallop
And go swing up on those bars.

'Then when you're finished swinging
We'll go further down the line
Where you'll sit in that contraption
And then start pumping iron.

'We will walk you on the treadmill
Until you go red in the face
And when you think you've had enough
I'll increase the walking pace.'

My clothes are wet and stuck to me
I'm sweating like a pig
When Joe came and by said, 'Loosen up,
Let's dance the Irish jig.'

Now I'm thinking where I would rather be
It's in the park under shady trees
As I crawl towards the shower room
On my hands and knobbly knees.

Two years have passed, Joe says to me,
'You're up among the best
You're looking like a man at last
Even growing hairs upon your chest.'

Now I strut up and down the beach
And show off all my brawn
And if a skinny weed goes by
I glare at him with scorn.

So if you are a weakling
Why don't you be like me
Get fit and trim at Old Joe's Gym
Where he'll make a man of thee.

"WHO CALLED THE MUG A REF ?"

# The footy match

We are going along a dusty track
Through spinifex and scrub
Heading towards a footy match
Played behind the Mataranka Pub.

This game is played but once a year
They come from far and wide
To see this famous battle fought
Playing twenty-five a side.

We play it on O'Reilley's patch
The cows have all been shifted
The bull has got a one-way trip
And the cow dungs all been lifted.

We've got the Sheikh from Scrubby Creek
And Jonno from Camp Crockets
They'll run the swy game on the side
And fill both their old hip pockets.

Now Killer Kane from Castlemaine
Said, 'I'll be the referee
I'll tame this mob of skinheads
Or I'll wrap them round a tree.'

The ref called them all together
And said, 'Listen good, you mugs,
There'll be no biting, kicking or scratching,
Or I'll pin back your flamin' lugs.'

The whistle blew, the ball was kicked
And up went a mighty cheer
Then O'Malley said, 'They'll kill me, mate,
Cos I forgot to chill the beer.'

They went into a huddle
What I think they call a scrum
Then grunt and groan and push like hell
While they smell each other's bum.

The game it seesawed back and forth
Neither side would give an inch
The stale grog it kept oozing out
But neither team were game to flinch.

The ref said, 'Steady on, you lot
Your tactics make me scream
Not only that, it's plain to see
I'm fast running out of steam.'

With the ref and whistle in low gear
The game slowed to a crawl
Until Murphy blacked O'Leary's eye
And caused an all-in brawl.

The fists they flew, the boots went in
Until most were lying prone
With bodies strewn around the patch
It resembled a battle zone.

So the ref blew on his whistle
And said, 'It's nil-all score
So I have no hesitation
Than to declare this game a draw.'

Then we sat the keg up on a stump
And knocked out the bottom bung
So the players said, 'Let's drink the lot
While we finish off our day of fun.'

So while we sip the amber ale
We quietly shed a tear
In remembrance of the days gone by
And hope we'll all be back next year.

# The cross-country race

We all lined up at the barbed wire fence
The weather it was fair
And all got down in a sprinter's crouch
As the starter's gun punctured the air.

We loped along towards halfway
When the leaders made a break
Then I kept getting further back
It was more than I could take.

The pace it was a cracker
I developed an awful thirst
And running up this two-mile hill
I thought my lungs would surely burst.

My feet were feeling leaden
As I plodded up this pull
When over the hill at breakneck speed
Came old Ernie Paton's bull.

My legs got into over-drive
As I thought this could be slaughter
I'll have to beat the good Lord's feat
Of when he walked across the water.

With lowered horns he charged at me
I thought my future rather bleak
There's only one way out of this
I'll have to swim across the creek.

I swam across to the other side
And lay down on the grass
When the bull appeared from nowhere
About to make his second pass.

I seemed to get a second wind
And instead of marking time
I took off in a cloud of dust
Towards the finishing line.

I galloped past the leaders
Doing twice their running pace
And fell across the finishing line
I had won the flamin' race.

So I stood up on a wooden box
Received my trophy made of wool
Now there's only one that I should thank
And that's old Ernie Paton's bull.

# The quake

Was about a week ago today
It was pretty lousy weather
When my old shack gave a little shake
It was what they call a tremor.

I looked around my sturdy home
It will last through thick and thin
It's built of good strong saplings
And sheets of corrugated tin.

So I'm settling down to go to bed
On this cold and frosty night
But I'm going to don my woolly socks
Before putting out the light.

It was just about the break of day
When my shack began to shake
I thought, My Gawd, it's on again
It's going to be another quake.

The ground was all a rumble
As what I built to last for years
Began to fall to pieces
And collapse around my ears.

Two possums living in the roof
Came crashing on my bed
One landed on his backside
The other landed on his head.

My shack it was a shambles
The floor began to crack
And the only thing left standing
Was the old dunny out the back.

I stood around amidst the calm
Waiting for the after shocks
On what used to be my doorstep
And wearing nothing but my socks.

My old cattle dog ran up a log
With his tail between his legs
And what I thought to be my gander
Started laying spotted eggs.

So I've put the billy on to boil
As I gaze out to the west
And it's now I sit and ponder
On what to do now for the best.

REBUILT A MANSION NOW, MATE.

To pack my swag and head back home
That's part of my dilemma
Or start and build another shack
And risk another tremor.

Well I've been here more than half my life
Underneath this cloudless sky
So I'll start and build another shack
Then I'll stay here till I die.

# The shearers

The cook's been up since three a.m.
Now he's about to ring the gong
Cos he's got a heap of tucker ready
To last the whole day long.

Old Spring Heeled Jack from up the track
Has sharpened up the shears
He knows his way around this shed
He's been here for fifty years.

The tally boards are hanging up
The tables all cleaned down
The boss is looking at his watch
While the shearers lounge around.

The roustabouts are all fired up
They have penned up all the sheep
The sheep dogs they have done their job
And now are going back to sleep.

Then Lofty Len from Rutherglen
Said I'll lay two to one
That Roddy the Rat from Ballarat
Will be this year's top gun.

Old Boozy Bob from Yorkeys Knob
Said, 'I'll have a piece of that
I'll put some dollars on myself
To beat the flamin' Rat.'

So Boozy Bob and Roddy the Rat
Got up to toe the line
The roustabouts and dogs woke up
It was time to rise and shine.

The whistle blew, it was the start
Their backs they were a-bending
The sheep were shorn in record time
And the line it was unending.

They went all day at a killer pace
Until their backs were sore
When the boss said, 'Right, your time is up
You've got a tied and even score.'

They insisted on a recount
And found Boozy ahead by one
So they all adjourned to Maloney's Pub
To finish off this day of fun.

It only took a drink or two
To loosen up the tongue
And then elaborate on what
These two jacky howes had done.

And when a shearer starts to brag
About what he's done all day
He can equal any fisherman
And the one that got away.

Now Boozy's gone and Roddy too
To the next shed due to shear
But they left behind their trademark
Until we shear again next year.

# The rodeo

Now I've joined the riders' circuit
It is the only way to go
So I'll saddle up and have a ride
At the Mount Isa rodeo.

The crush is set, the rails are up
The ground is rough and ready
For all who care to try their luck
On a wild and bucking neddy.

Now Dirty Bill from up the hill
Said, 'I'm here to try my luck
Just poke him good right in the ribs
To make sure that he can buck.'

I looked around at all the nags
Until I found a likely colt
I said, 'I'll try my luck on him
His name was Thunderbolt.'

I got up on his bony back
To stay on was a must
But he put his head between his knees
And I landed head first in the dust.

Then I got up on a flighty nag
In all new cowboy gear
And went all out at breakneck speed
To lasso a galloping steer.

I got the rope around his horns
And tried to jerk him round
But all that I accomplished
Was to drag my backside on the ground.

So I had a look at what was left
Then said, 'Let me have a go
I'll have a ride on Chainsaw
And put up a mighty show.'

Now Chainsaw is a Brahma Bull
He's the meanest of the few
With massive chest and solid rump
And short legs that barely grew.

He let me get up on his back
Then bounded out the shute
I landed full length on my face
I must have looked a damn galoot.

Then added to this insult
He stomped around my ear
Then gave a final farewell snort
As he horned me in the rear.

Well I think I've learned my lesson
This rough riding's for the mugs
So I'll stick to riding my rocking horse
Where I can fall down on the rugs.

"THINK I'M IN THE GRIP OF GRIP OF THE GROG, MATE!"

# Dusty's pub

We are going to stop along the track
To try and quench our thirst
We'll just stop off at Dusty's pub
It's the one we get to first.

We are miles and miles from anywhere
This is the real outback
As we wend our dusty way up north
Along the famous Birdsville Track.

Tis Dusty Lane who owns the pub
He's been there for many a year
And well known in this territory
To fill you full of cheer.

The pub is very hard to find
It's off the beaten track
A few sheets of corrugated iron
Just like a miner's shack.

There's another shack around the back
Where you can make a camp
But there isn't any power
You have to light the Tilley lamp.

The barmaid is a female roo
Keeps the money in her pouch
And when she's finished serving grog
She puts her feet up on the couch.

Well, we drank a couple of stubbies
And were about to ask for more
When a massive great red kangaroo
Came hopping through the door.

He downed a stubbie of Fosters
You could tell he'd been here before
Cos he gave a piercing whistle
And in hopped seven more.

A cockatoo flew in just then
Along with a grey galah
And they sampled all the stubbies
As they strolled along the bar.

A goanna came in from the scrub
Drank a stubbie through a straw
While the emu swallowed a Foster's can
Then passed out on the floor.

The front door burst wide open
In waltzed a feral pig
Which gulped a couple of tinnies
Then danced an Irish jig.

The wombat he fell off his stool
Had drunk more than he could take
And flaked out in a corner
Was a six-foot tiger snake.

The brolga did his love dance
He was like a wind-up toy
And the magpie started singing
'The Wild Colonial Boy'.

The barmaid scratched behind her ear
Said, 'He won't come through that door,'
As the dingo howled out in the scrub
He had been banned the night before.

The pelican said, 'Fill me up,
Five stubbies in my beak
Then I'll fly home to the missus
And the kids at Scrubby Creek.'

I was about to order another drink
Murphy said, 'My Gawd, I'm off the grog,'
Cos on the bar and facing him
Was a dirty big green frog.

As the bar was getting crowded
I thought it time to venture forth
So we staggered out into the heat
And continued heading north.

We stopped in the town of Boulia
And were in the Workers' Club
When Murphy started talking
About our stop at Dusty's pub.

He said, 'I thought the grog had got to me
Cos I've drunk both near and far
But first time I've ever sat and drank
With a green frog on the bar.'

# The cricket match

We have gathered here from near and far
Now the football season's over
The cricket starts at ten am
On O'Reilley's patch of clover.

We have mowed and shaped the wicket
We've got our boots and hats
Our shirts are out of mothballs
And we found the ball and bats.

The wombats they are two to one
Our galahs are even money
As we toss the coin to see who bats
On this field of milk and honey.

The coin was flipped, we won the toss
And sent the wombats in to bat
Then the umpire said, 'You'll have to wait
Until I find my flamin' hat.'

So we scattered all around the ground
All prepared this ball to chase
As our Wing'y Bell came up to bowl
At his fast to medium pace.

Now Wing'y has started his run up
And what an awesome sight
Six-foot-five and one long arm
And black as a winter's night.

"GAWD, THE POMS BEAT US AGAIN !"

The first ball bowled was just a blur
The keeper said, 'Howzat?'
The umpire said, 'You'll have to go
Cos you didn't move your bat.'

The next ball was much slower
And was hit with a mighty slog
To be fielded on the boundary
By Paddy Murphy's mangy dog.

He ran off towards the township
As he galloped through the scrub
Then found an open doorway
Into the Ettimogah Pub.

We chased him into a corner
Then gave a mighty cheer
As the umpire said, 'It's early yet
So we've got time to have a beer.

The time it passed so quickly
We were on a wacky wicket
So we think we'll have just one more drink
Then go and play some cricket.

Well, we all got in position
When the umpire said, 'There's trouble
Cos every time I look down there
I'm seeing flamin' double.'

His old knees they did a buckle
His eyes were glazed and dim
So we tossed him in the cowshed
That's the last we'll see of him.

Then we folded up the cricket gear
And stored the lot away
Until we organise our other match
Which we play on New Year's Day.

# Anzac Day

## A tribute to the Australian fighting forces

On the twenty-fifth of April
It's a great day for Australia
To see the old proud Diggers march
In all their fine regalia.

We were a new-born nation
When the British gave the call,
'We need you in South Africa
Where we have our backs against the wall.'

As yet an untried fighter
We soon became a mighty force
When we saddled up our brumbies
And became the Aussie First Light Horse.

We fought from out the trenches
On the blood-soaked Flanders dells
Then went to face up to the Turks
At the dreaded Dardanelles.

We fought them in Gallipoli
And the battle of the Somme
In fact there wasn't any place
When we didn't tag along.

The Germans did their level best
To hold onto all they took
And twice we had to liberate
That place they call Tobruk.

We flew in the Battle of Britain
We fought in the Coral Sea
We slogged it up the Kokoda Trail
Where no man ought to be.

Another call from overseas
From the country of Vietnam
There to face a raging battle
For the village of Long Tan.

They took us from all walks of life
We wore our battledress with pride
A bit rough round the edges
But we took all in our stride.

We proved a fearsome fighter
Always very hard to beat
And when the chips were really down
We were not known to retreat.

Now with each year gone it takes its toll
Along with the daily grind
But we always put this day aside
For the mates we left behind.

Some say I'll march the route
There's some say I'll refrain
I still would like to join my mates
But now I use a walking cane.

Then we gather at the RSL
And while having an ale or two
We tell our tales of yesteryear
To old mates that are true blue.

Then as the day draws to a close
And the sun begins to set
That's when we hold a minute's silence—
LEST WE FORGET.

# My ambition

I left off school before my time
Because I was too dumb to get a pass
But my teacher said, 'You'll do all right
You're the lowest in the class.'

So I travelled to the city
I thought, here I'll make the grade
But I found it hard to get a job
Because I'm too dumb to learn a trade.

Well, I stuck it out a few more years
Was always on the dole
While I tried a few more tactics
To stop living like a mole.

I tried to blow my bugle
And become a jazz musician
But found I'm no damn good at that
So I became a politician.

I took my soapbox to the park
And for endless days did natter
While people stopped to listen in
To my words of idle chatter.

A politician passed one day
Said, 'Hey mate, you're doing fine
I'll get you in the Upper House
And you'll be a mate of mine.'

So I sat there in the Upper House
Then I knew I had got it right
I'll make the grade in this here job
Because I can neither read nor write.

Out there are many idiots
Who work and pay their tax
I'll get my hands on some of that
Because the Treasury's pretty lax.

I'll buy myself a brand new Rolls
It will be a Silver Cloud
I don't want any make-believe
I want to stand out in a crowd.

I'll go overseas and buy my clothes
They'll all be in the latest fashion
Then I'll holiday in the south of France
It's only government cheques I'm cashin'.

Now how to run this country
Well, we had a big debate
Going to borrow fifty million bucks
And put it on the slate.

We will give ourselves another raise
Then hang on in suspension
Because we'll all be in retirement soon
On our parliamentary pension.

Well, now I'm on my pension
But the bills they are unending
So on just five thousand bucks a week
I will have to curb my spending.

If you find it hard to get a job
You do not need tuition
All you do is talk like hell
And become a politician.

# A camping weekend

We left our home one early morn
Went around the city fountains
And took a track that led us west
Towards the lofty mountains.

We drove along for many miles
Until we came upon a park
Now we have to go on foot from here
And try and beat the dark.

We got out all the camping gear
Put our packs up on our back
Then started out to hike more miles
On a worn and dusty track.

We had only hiked a mile or two
When we saw a cockatoo
And standing just ahead of us
Was an old grey kangaroo.

He eyed us off for quite a while
Then quietly hopped aside
While we took off up the track again
With the mountains as our guide.

We were getting tired and weary
When we heard a bellbird call
Then just around the bend ahead
We came upon a waterfall.

We dropped our packs down on the ground
Made camp here by the stream
With nice clear water running by
It's a city dweller's dream.

We sat around the camp fire
And watched the billy boil
Thinking about our friends back home
About to start their nightly toil.

We listened to the rippling stream
It was a very pleasant sound
And we thought of our location
Where the wildlife does abound.

We settled down for a peaceful night
When we got a painful sting
Was the mozzie squadron leader
On his usual nightly fling.

He said, 'You're right for stinging,'
So he brought the flight along
And the flapping of their tiny wings
Set up their battle song.

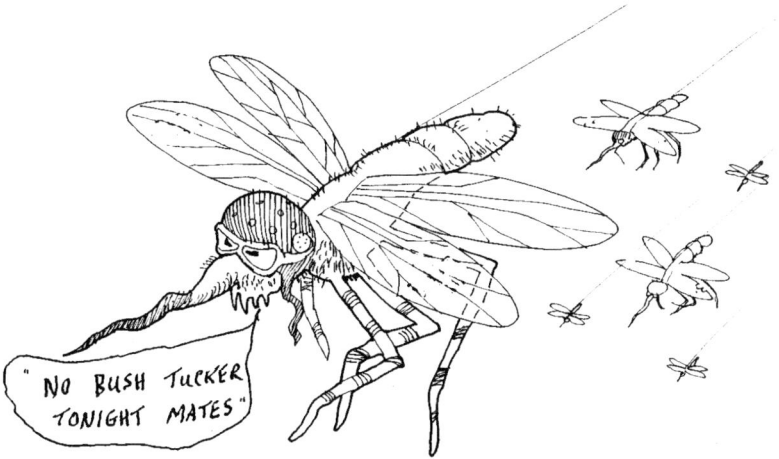

They peeled off in formation
Their stings all at the ready
And landed with precision
While their leader kept them steady.

We crawled out in the morning
After a very sleepless night
All covered with red blotches
We were a pitiful sight.

Now we are heading homeward
Back to our city push
You can keep your flamin' wildlife
In your mozzie-ridden bush.

# The Capricornia barge

We are leaving the port of Townsville
And taking an entourage
To go to Magnetic Island
So we have to go by barge.

We rang up for a booking
We're told the coast was clear
And that we would be departing
Before the end of year.

I questioned our mode of travel
As I picked up my boarding pass
So a female voice politely said,
'You're all going tourist class.'

We lined up at the barrier
The skipper said, 'We're running late
Now as you're backing down the ramp
Don't overshoot the gate.'

The barge was fully laden
And we gave a mighty cheer
As the whistle blew, the gate was raised
And we were leaving here.

The motors whined, the revs built up
The barge got up a sway
But full four knots against the tide
We weren't making any way.

As we left the Aussie shore behind
The old barge gave a shudder
The skipper said, 'My Gawd, I think
We've lost the flamin' rudder.'

So we were going around in circles
And out about mid-stream
When the motors gave a final cough
We had just run out of steam.

So we all got out the paddles
We're set for a good two-hour row
When a bloke came by in a tinnie
And said, 'I'll take you under tow.'

Well, we landed on the island
And gave a good report
To all who care to listen
At the Horseshoe Bay Resort.

Now if you want an island holiday
And take an entourage
We can very highly recommend
The old Capricornia barge.

# The local show

The old town's come to life again
All the folks are on the go
Getting ready all their wares
To exhibit at the show.

The farmers come from far and wide
By cart, by van and trailer
While the show boss starts his monologue
On his battered old loudhailer.

There's billy goats and horses
There's cows and poddies too
There's ducks and geese and laying hens
and the occasional cockatoo.

They all are looking spick and span
They're curry-combed and groomed
The roosters strut around with pride
Showing how they're richly plumed.

The sideshows are arriving
It looks just like a rally
As they set up their contraptions
At the back of Sideshow Alley.

There's the carousel and dodgems
Take a ride on the Ferris wheel
And you can't mistake the octopus
Because it makes the lassies squeal.

The spruiker at the boxing tent
Said, 'You can make a buck or two
Just last three rounds with Punch Drunk Pete
Or the bloke from Woolloomooloo.'

See Two Ton Tess or good Queen Bess
There's double-jointed Jake
See Tiny Tim the Tattooed Dwarf
Or the double-headed snake.

Now we've had the final judging
As we watch the grand parade
Of all the country livestock
Followed up by a motorcade.

So now we start to plan ahead
That will keep us on the go
Until we all come back and meet next year
At our old town's annual show.

# First visit to Sydney from Humpty Dump cattle station

We left our Dump about mid-year
This big city to explore
And travelled here to Sydney
Because we ain't been here before.

We got off the train at Central
And must have looked a bunch of hicks
Because we ain't city slickers
We're just people from the sticks.

Our eyes lit up in wonder
As we gazed around in awe
At this massive concrete jungle
From the roof down to the floor.

We stood upon the sidewalk
And could not believe our eyes
Because of these tall buildings
We could hardly see the skies.

We strolled around old Sydney Town
And took in all the sights
From Luna Park beneath the bridge
To the famous harbour lights.

We saw some creatures sitting round
They even resembled humans too
But if we saw them sitting in the bush
We would toss them in a zoo.

We found a place to rest a while
Trying to ease our aching feet
But a copper said, 'Right, move along
You're blocking up the street.'

So we had to walk along the path
At twice our normal pace
And make just like a city-ite
With no expression on the face.

We went to a game of football
And what a game of hate
All we heard from go to woe
Was 'Kill the buggers, mate.'

The whistles blow, the sirens wail
The traffic is chaotic
Another week in this here town
And we'll all be on narcotics.

Well, we are not impressed with Sydney
So we're going to leave this push
And go back home to settle down
In our own beloved bush.

Now to all of you in Sydney
There's an open invitation
Come to the bush and visit us
On an outback cattle station.

# A city-ite's visit to Humpty Dump cattle station

I'm leaving town. I'm outward bound
I've accepted an invitation
To see what life is all about
On this outback cattle station.

I got on a train to take me north
And got off at Townsville Station
To take a branch line way out west
And find this bush creation.

I boarded a steaming hulk of rust
They said, 'It's called the rattler,'
The fireman said, 'She'll get there, mate
She's the original Aussie Battler.'

They let me off at a whistle stop
I said, 'Where do I find this dump?
They said, 'Follow your nose, it's a few mile out
Just beyond the old Black Stump.'

I was greeted on arrival
By ferocious dogs and growls
So I stood frozen on the spot
And hoped I wouldn't use my bowels.

The boss came out and rescued me
Said, 'Cripes, you're kinda white
Is that a Sydney suntan
Or did you nearly die of fright?'

Well, we went to bed at sundown
I had hoped to sleep all night
But soon the boss was shaking me
While he lit the flaming light.

Said, 'Come on, mate, we're running late
To harness up the ploughs
Cos when we're finishing ploughing
Then you can go and milk the cows.

'You've got to feed the horses
Feed the chooks and poddies too
Then go find yourself a shovel
And clean out the outback loo.

'Help the missus with the washing
Hang the clothes up on the line
And if you drag them in the dirt
You'll feel this boot of mine.

'Right here there's miles of country
Right to that mountain side
It's too damn far for you to walk
So you'll have to learn to ride.'

They sat me on the old grey mare
And she took off like a rocket
I landed in a pile of dust
Right on my old hip pocket.

With blistered hands and aching back
I took off my dirty boots
I can't take any more of this
I'm worn down to the boots.

So I've packed my gear and I'm heading out
Back towards the city push
Cos it ain't no life for a city-ite
In this Godforsaken bush.

# The golfer

Now I'm getting close to middle age
And I don't look all that trim
So I'll have to find a pastime
That will keep me sleek and slim.

I went into a sports store
Took my time to browse around
While trying to find a hobby
That keeps two feet on the ground.

After many hours browsing
And a visit to two pubs
I decided to take up playing golf
So I'll buy a set of clubs.

Now I really look the golfing pro
Plus fours and golfing cap
And a wee instruction booklet
To tell me where I'm at.

I was on the golf course early
Before the bellbirds call
The booklet said the first thing now
You've got to address the ball.

So I said, 'Listen, pill, see yonder hill
That's where you'll finish up
Cos from here to there in four short strokes
I should have you in the cup.'

Now, having addressed the little ball
And with two feet on the ground
I had to wriggle my backside
Without making a flamin' sound.

I probed around and finally found
My two iron I did bring
Then kept my eye upon the ball
As I took a backward swing.

I hit that ball with all my might
And I cannot tell a fib
I nearly dislocated my shoulder
And I lapped a lower rib.

The ball rolled off its little tee
A full two feet, no more
I thought, there's no-one looking,
So I won't add this to my score.

After ploughing a trench with my two iron
I threw the ball into the scrub
And then in a fit of temper
I broke the handle of the club.

I've given up playing this game of golf
I'll not become a golfing laddie
But I'll still be there for the exercise
I've just become a golfing caddie.

# The jillaroo

I was bought up in a country town
Where there wasn't much to do
So had to leave and get a job
I became a jillaroo.

My parents wished me best of luck
Said, 'We both think that you're wacky
But no matter where you hang your hat
You'll always be our daughter Jacky.'

So I packed my gear and headed west
Towards the land of flies and dust
Of good red earth and spinifex
To get a riding job or bust.

I was getting pretty weary
As I staggered up the track
And my shoulders were a'sagging
With the knapsack on my back.

I looked towards the setting sun
And with grim determination
Kept plodding on towards my goal
To find a cattle station.

Two guys stopped by in a battered truck
Said, 'If you like to climb up too
We will take you home to meet the boss,
He's in need of a jillaroo.'

"RECKON I'M THE NUMBER ONE STOCKMAN!"

The boss he looked me up and down
Then said, 'Yes I think you'll do
Let's kit you out in boots and hat
And make you look like a jillaroo.

'Now go over there to the break-in pen
Let Charlie be your guide
He'll put you up on a quarter horse
And teach you how to ride.'

He legged me onto the saddle
Then started to lead me round
But I landed on my derriere
And bounced along the ground.

The ringers they all had a laugh
Then said, 'Get back up on his back
Cos if you let him beat you now
You can walk back down the track.'

It took a couple of days or more
To get into my stride
Then Charlie said, 'Now off you go
And show us how to ride.'

I left the ranch at breakneck speed
They way ahead was clear
Til I topped a rise and came across
This long-horned rebel steer.

I took off in a cloud of dust
My long hair it was flying
I caught that steer in record time
And I wasn't even trying.

I herded that steer back to the ranch
Put him into a cattle yard
Then Wall Eyed Tim, the cattle dog
Took his usual place on guard.

The ringers said, 'That's well done, mate
You have passed with flying colours
Now you're a first-class jillaroo
You can muster with us fellows.'

With the monsoon season close at hand
We will beat the northerly buster
And leave the ranch without delay
For the yearly cattle muster.

The days were long and tiring
Was fourteen days or more
That we stood up in the stirrups
Cos we all got saddle sore.

So we culled them from the muster
Then sang a sweet refrain
As we drove them off for market
To the nearest cattle train.

A city guy was at the train
Asked me, 'Is it riding all you do?'
I said, 'All day, mate, from dawn till dusk
I am the station's jillaroo.'

He looked at me and scratched his head
Said 'I'm from the city and it's true
I always thought that what you are
Was a female kangaroo.'

A few years now have come and gone
I have mustered with the best
The boss said, 'Right, you've served your time
Now enjoy a well earned rest.'

To all young girls without a job
This could be your salvation
So pack your bag and head out west
Till you find a cattle station.

The work is quite rewarding
It's the best thing you could do
And I am talking from experience
I have been a station JILLAROO.

# A visit to England

We departed from Australia
With all new gear to wear
And headed west to England
Flying with Malaysian Air.

It took twenty hours flying time
And we were feeling kind of rough
When an English voice said, 'Breathe in, folks
You've been down under long enough.'

We got a train on the yellow circle
And alighted at St James
Then had to walk for half a mile
Before we reached the muddy Thames.

We went to the famous Tower
Saw Sir Walter Raleigh's bed
Then went upstairs to find the place
Where they lopped off Mary's head.

We thought that we were seeing things
It was an Old Beefeater Guard
As we made our way along the street
To the famous Scotland Yard.

"JUST CAME UP FROM DOWN UNDER."

We paid a visit to the Wax Works
And what a revelation
They bring the past back to real life
With all their wax creation.

Some figures fill you full of awe
Some fill you full of sorrows
And then it makes your blood run cold
When you're in the House of Horrors.

We gained entry into the House of Lords
Where the brains of England meet
Though all the people seem to think
That their brains are in their seat.

We asked a London bobby
Where do we find Big Ben?
He looked at us and scratched his head,
'Try Downing Street, Number Ten.'

We took a bus out to the West
Where we hoped to find the source
Of the famous English legend
Lady Godiva and her horse.

She looked so lovely sitting there
In her long and golden tresses
I said, 'My dear, you're tanned and bare,'
She said, 'That's because I don't wear dresses.'

Now we are going south to Bath
While we are on the go
And then see Drakie playing bowls
Down on the Plymouth Hoe.

Then we travel back to London Town
Once more to venture forth
We will have rest here overnight
Before a coach tour of the north.

# A Scottish tour

It is time to leave old London Town
We will travel by Trafalgar Tour
We will soon be pulling out of here
To where we haven't been before.

We are heading north to Scotland
Going close to Inverness
Where we hope to see the monster
In that pond they call Loch Ness.

We arrived at bonnie Glasgow
Though it wasn't a Saturday night
We managed to down a couple of drinks
Before putting out the light.

An overnight stop at Fort William
Then visited the Isle of Skye
Where we hoped to find a distillery
And sample a dram of rye.

And while up here in Scotland
I would love to solve a riddle
What does a Scottie have beneath his kilt
Somewhere just below his middle?

Queen Mary knew the answer
She had the Scotties all worked out
She used a mirror facing up
And it didn't leave her in any doubt.

But now I have found the answer
And I'll tell it just to thee
I found out quite by accident
He has the same damn things as me.

We are going back through Nottingham
So I want to see that famous wood
And meet up with a mate of mine
His name is Robin Hood.

I would like to meet old Friar Tuck
And the Maid Marian too
Then find that lousy Sheriff
And send him back to Timbuktu.

We have just arrived in London
And it's shortly after four
So we'll try and catch up on some sleep
Before we begin another tour.

# A European coach tour

Once again we are on the move
We can't sit still and rust
So are going with Trafalgar Tours
They are a mob that we can trust.

We've come from all around the world
There's Yanks and Springboks too
And some from way down under
From the land of the kangaroo.

Now Robert's in the driver's seat
Our lives are in his hands
As he operates this tour coach
While we pass through many lands.

Our captain read the riot act
So we all know where we're at
His speech was quite impressive
He was talking through his hat.

We have left the port of Dover
Having left that massive traffic jam
And now we hope to find the highway
That will lead to Amsterdam.

Our timetable it is all worked out
So we have to toe the line
We get a respite through the night
Until it's time to rise and shine.

We leave the bed at breakneck speed
Then try and beat even time
To pack our gear and get downstairs
Where we just have time to dine.

Then it's face up to the elements
Battle cold and then the heat
As we clamber up aboard the coach
Then try and find a flamin' seat.

We spend many hours on this seat
One could hardly call a throne
And wish by three o'clock
That they were down and lying prone.

Now we've travelled many miles this tour
And many miles we've had to walk
We are nearly worn down to the knees
Like the proverbial family stork.

We have beaten all the odds it's true
And we all emerged a winner
As we gather round this one last time
To enjoy a farewell dinner.

Now we are back in London
Having said our last goodbyes
So we'll point our nose towards our home
As we flit across the skies.

# A quick tour of Australia

We are departing from north Queensland
Going south then east to west
To travel through each Aussie State
And see which one we like the best.

We are heading out through Winton
Towards the great outback
There to see Matilda waltzing
Along a hard and dusty track.

Then visit the town of Longreach
See the Stockman's Hall of Fame
Before we arrive in Brisbane
Where we will see a football game.

At Tweed Heads we cross the border
And with the wind behind our tails
We reach the town of Lismore
So are now in New South Wales.

It is here we cross the great divide
And with Sydney down the track
We will find a place to rest awhile
And hang our hats up on a rack.

A westerly trip to the mountains blue
Where we sat up on a ridge
Then looked down on Sydney Town
And the famous Harbour Bridge.

Then going east from Albury
Through eighty miles of scrub
We landed on the doorstep
Of the Dora Dora Pub.

Here we cross the Murray River
Where we haven't crossed before
Then drive along the highway
Through the town of Mangalore.

We are heading south to Melbourne
As we pass along this way
Where they say it's not unusual
To have four seasons in one day.

We are passing through the mallee
And its lovely sunny skies
Where the cockatoos fly backwards
To keep the dust out of their eyes.

We have sighted the city of Adelaide
Where the Torrens River flows
In the State of South Australia
And renown for its crows.

Through the dust to Coober Pedy
It's a town of many holes
Where the townsfolk all live underground
Like a bunch of flamin' moles.

There we start to cross the Nullarbor
It's Australia's greatest plain
And it's only fools who drive across
All the sane folk go by train.

We travel through the goldfields
On our westward trek to Perth
Then head out north through Wydgee
And a very barren earth.

We go across the Carnarvon range
Then up through Bulloo Downs
And all the while still going north
We don't pass through many towns.

Our journey's almost over
As we pass through the town of Broome
Then head due east to Darwin
And we can't get there too soon.

Our last leg takes us southwards
Down through Tennant Creek
Then across to the Queensland border
There our homeward trail we seek.

It was a mammoth journey
Of at least twelve thousand k's
And the whole trip took from go to woe
A time of thirty days.

Now after all that travelling
We will enjoy a well earned rest
Then pass to you our judgment
On what State we thought the best.

# The alley cat

A tabby puss came into town
His Christian name is Batt
He hasn't got a pedigree
He's just a small-time alley cat.

He said to all the cats in town,
'I'm not looking for a fight
But I want to join your little gang
And make a catty noise at night.'

So the locals held a meeting
Said, 'This bloke's got no show
We'll bring in Punch Drunk Ginger Mick
And show this cat where to go.'

Now Mick's an old campaigner
He's had many an alley fight
And when he's got his hackles up
He is an awesome sight.

He gets into a boxer's crouch
Then swears and yowls and spits
While sizing up his opponent
And where to land his well-timed hits.

Now Batt's no backyard brawler
But won't take a backward step
So punch on, Mick, and do your worst
While you're feeling full of pep.

So they circled one another
Then stood there face to face
As Ginger Mick said, 'Okay, Batt,
I'm going to liven up the pace.'

Then Mick lashed out with a vicious right
Caught Batty on the hip
So Batt said, 'Keep your punches up
Or I'll split your bottom lip.'

Batt threw a couple of punches
They all made Mickey swear
Then every time Mick threw a punch
Young Batty wasn't there.

Then Batt unsheathed his catty claws
And landed on Mickey's back
So the fur it started flying
As they wrestled down the track.

Soon Mick gave up the struggle
Batt said, 'Now I've worn you down
You're no longer the alley champion
You're just an old back-alley clown.'

Then Batt lined up the locals
And said, 'Now I'll sort you out
Just get in line for a punch up
Or a two- or three-round bout.'

Well, Batt couldn't get a punch up
But was told, 'Now you can join our alley
Just make your peace with Ginger Mick
Then we'll hold a back yard rally.'

Now that Batt has joined the alley gang
His future seems much brighter
But no-one's game to wise them up
That Batt's an outback titled fighter.

# The place that never was

Am leaving the south for parts unknown
Having accepted an invitation
To spend my annual holiday
On an outback cattle station.

I took the route through Broken Hill
Went along the Birdsville Track
Amidst the scrub and spinifex
This is the real outback.

I crossed the Northern Territory border
At a place called Abimonga
There asked an old bloke how to find
This cattle station 'Linga Longa'.

The old chap sat and scratched his head
Said, 'Now this here place you seek
I am not too sure so will have a guess
It's way out west of Tennant Creek.

'So follow this track to yonder hill
Where the Afghan had his camel train
And the grey galahs fly backwards
To keep their eyes out of the rain.

'Then go along at a steady pace
For a day and a half, no more
That's where there was a dog-proof fence
And a big artesian bore.

'There used to be an old shack there
Before the white ants ate it down
But it's hard to find the white ants now
They're all gone underground.

'If you follow this fence for eighty miles
You'll see ten trees in a clump
That's where there used to be a bottle
Stuck in a burnt and blackened stump.

'It's here the water boils in the water bag
And the roos roam fancy free
So point your nose towards the north
From where the old windmill used to be.

'You keep going in this direction
Until you find a bottle tree
That's where they hung the Chinaman
In eighteen eighty-three.

'It's from here you travel westwards
Through bulldust thick and thin
Until you come across what's not there now
It was an old pub built of tin.

'Then when you see the min min lights
You are pretty close to home
But don't go trying to ring them up
They were never on the phone.'

I have located all these landmarks
So think I'm going fairly well
As I prepare to sleep beneath the stars
In my own five-star hotel.

Am looking forward to my arrival
Where they don't sit still and rust
And have the bushies' three-course meal
Of tinned dog damper and dust.

Now as I approach the homestead fence
I can see an old log shack
And then I see an Afghan
Lead his camels round the back.

There's a mob of big red kangaroos
All roaming fancy free
And then I see a Chinaman
Hanging from the bottle tree.

I enter through the old wood gate
But the yard is all too clean
And all I find is a vacant block
Where the old homestead should have been.

I should try and backtrack to the south
But I can't do that because
I have yet to awaken from this dream
To find the place that never was.

# The astronaut

I have now become an astronaut
So am going up into space
Where I'll be among the Martians
Meeting with them face to face.

They said I had to undergo
A rigorous training course
Cos when I leave the Earth behind
There's no gravitational force.

I had to give up drinking beer
To give up smoking was a must
So when I go up into space
I'll just sit still and rust.

They put me in a monkey suit
Shoved a glass bowl on my head
And then to keep me weighted down
A pair of gum boots made of lead.

They sat me in this contraption
Was like an over-sized cigar
And pointed up towards the sky
Where we find the evening star.

"THINK I'M MOON STUCK MATE?"

I was just about to take a nap
When there was this mighty roar
Then my large cigar shot upwards
And my feet went through the floor.

I thought, the way I'm going
I should pass Mars pretty soon
But my navigation went astray
And I landed on the moon.

I thought while here I'll go outside
And take a stroll around
But I found it hard on this here turf
To keep two feet on the ground.

I took a step with one foot first
And then I tried the two
Then found that I could bound along
Like a big red kangaroo.

So I got back in my spaceship
And pressed the starting gear
But the motor didn't spring to life
And I looked like staying here.

Then I got into a panic
As I gazed around my room
Cos one place I didn't want to be
Was hanging off the moon.

I shook this craft with all my might
And was overcome with mirth
As we broke away and began to fall
Towards good old mother Earth.

Our speed increased, we were just a blur
The old ship got the shakes
I frantically searched but failed to find
Some way to apply the brakes.

The Earth was rushing up at me
I was bathed in perspiration
How to stop this swift descent
I was at the point of desperation.

I was tangled in the bed clothes
And was halfway out of bed
When the missus grabbed my ankles
To stop me falling on my head.

She said, 'I think you had a nightmare
So I have tried to hold the fort
While you were here in orbit
Making like an astronaut.'

# A country courtship

I thought with whiskers on my chin
That I had grown up
I had even joined the work force
Though I'm still a playful pup.

So I thought it was time to look around
And take notice of the girls
Cos they seem to differ from us boys
Their hair is full of curls.

How would I go about this, mate?
Would they think I'm rather silly
If I fronted one and boldly asked
How would you like to be my filly?

So I looked around and finally found
A girl who took my fancy
I shyly said, 'My name is Fred,'
She said, 'My folks call me Nancy.'

We sat around and talked a while
My heart was all aflutter
I tried to ask her to be my girl
But all I did was stutter.

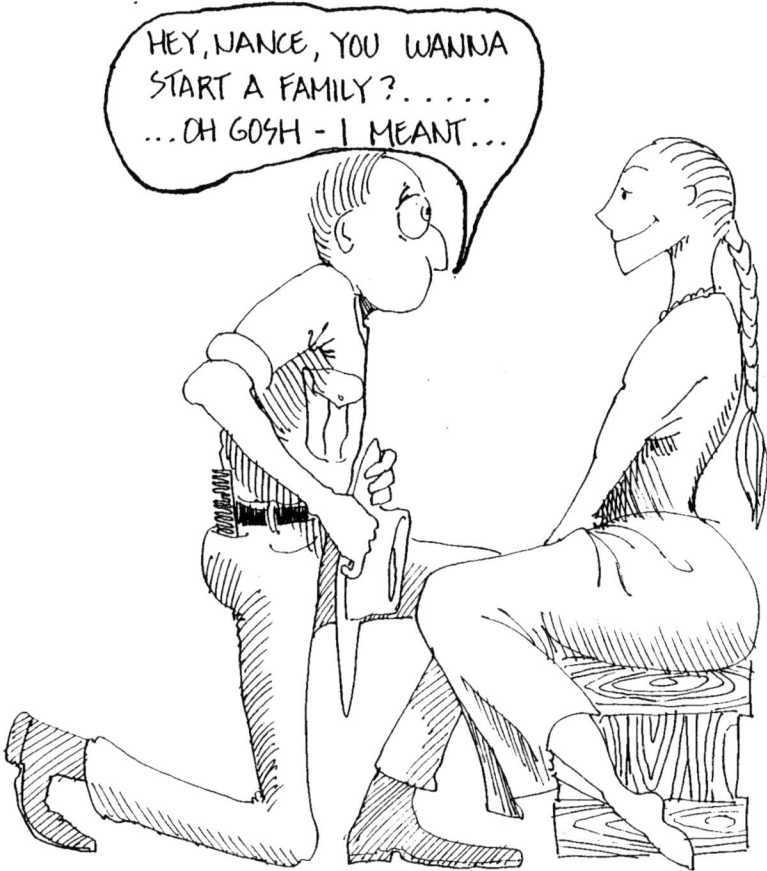

She lived out on her parents' farm
As the crow flies, thirty miles
I said, 'That's okay, I'll ride my bike
And turn up full of smiles.'

We held hands behind the cow shed
While gazing at the moon
And being just so close to her
By cripes, I thought I'd swoon.

I wooed her for a good long while
And our lives were full of bliss
Then one night I got real bold
And eventually stole a kiss.

She looked at me with starry eyes
And said, 'Good on yer, Fred
Why did it take you so damn long?
I had given you up for dead.'

So on bended knee I shyly asked,
'Nance, will you be my wife?'
She said, 'I will, you great big oaf
Now I'll be yours for life.'

So we hotted up the courtin' pace
And said we cannot tarry
'I'll get permission from your folks
To see if we can marry.'

Her daddy said, 'You're a good boy, Fred
She's yours with both our blessing
Now name a date to tie the knot
And save us all from guessing.'

After twenty years of wedded bliss
We feel life's just beginning
Add another forty years to that
And we will have had a damn good inning.

Now if you're young and single
And thinking of a wife
Don't rush it, boys, just take your time
Then you'll have a wife for life.

# A Xmas letter to Mary in the UK

Once again the time has come
To wish you all good cheer
While here in Far North Queensland
We will have our bellies full of beer.

As we are way Down Under
And you're in the upper seat
Where you'll have an icy Xmas
While we have ours in the heat.

We have our scorching temperatures
Along with the flies and dust
But we can go from place to place
While you sit still and rust.

You rug up like an Eskimo
All your winter clothes to wear
And then for six months hibernate
Like an Arctic polar bear.

And when it starts to snow again
On top of all the frost
You walk outside and turn around
Then find out that you're lost.

We walk outside and shade our eyes
To try and beat the glare
And then to beat the perspiration
We strip down to Adam's wear.

Our ducks and turkeys roam around
They are always on the loose
And with a summer Christmas
We don't even cook the goose.

We will have a seafood platter
And a nice cold salad plate
While you stuff down a big hot meal
Then whinge about your weight.

You boast about your Pommy land
Your cities full of smog
And then when Xmas come along
You can't see them for the fog.

But we will think of you on Xmas Day
And toast you with a beer
And wish you all the best of luck
For the new and coming year.

# The circus

I've reached the age to leave off school
But things ain't what they seem
So I think I'll join the circus
It's a young school leaver's dream.

I went and found the circus boss
I said, 'I'm all fired up and ready
To join up with your circus
And have a job that's steady.'

'What can you do?' the ring boss asked,
'Can you juggle this or that?
Can you walk along a tightrope?
Or high dive into a vat?

'Go get yourself a scrubbing brush
Then find a water billy
A gallon of detergent soap
Then go and scrub down Milly.'

Now Milly is the family pet
She's the one they all adore
With two big ears and a six-foot trunk
And weighs three tons or more.

The first week went without a hitch
I thought this job a breeze
Until the ring boss calmly said,
'Now get up on that trapeze.'

I said, 'Listen, boss, I like this job
And I would like to stick around
But there's little hope of doing that
With my two feet off the ground.'

'You've got to pull your weight round here
So I've got to try you out
Go over there, see trainer Jim
He will sort you out, no doubt.'

Now trainer Jim's a tamer
He likes to tame big cats
Goes in a cage with several lions
And puts them through their acts.

He said, 'Come in, son, and have some fun
With these few great big moggies.'
'No thanks, trainer Jim,' says I
'I would much rather play with doggies.'

Now the circus is departing
As it goes from place to place
And I'm left on the sidewalk
With a forlorn look on my face.

The circus boss said, 'So long, son
This job ain't what it seems
And I'm only very sorry
We had to shatter all your dreams.'

# The Aussie Navy

I have always had the urge to go
And visit a foreign shore
Those far-off lands I dreamt about
Where I've never been before.

So now I've joined the navy
I'll wear the suit of navy blue
And climb about the rigging
Like all good sailors do.

They sent me down to Cerebos
To learn the why's and what's
But all I seem to ever learn
Was how to get tied up tying knots.

Then I strolled aboard my future home
It was a twenty-eight sail clipper
And I'm going to be the bosun's mate
Because I am the artful nipper.

They said, 'Let's weigh the anchor
And then unfurl the sails.'
But I couldn't weigh the anchor
Because I couldn't find the scales.

Now we have to have a lookout
It's in the crow's nest you will be
Because we will be a'hunting
On this wild and restless sea.

So point her nose toward the north
Keep her steady as she blows
Now I had better go up topside
And find a nest among the crows.

After many days of shore leave
The ship became a wreck
So I had to find some cleaning gear
And start swabbing down the deck.

I eventually found the padre
But I didn't like his tone
When he said, 'My son, what do you want?'
I said, 'I want your holy stone.'

They said, 'You take the second watch,'
Now I'm in a state of shock
I couldn't find a second watch
I couldn't even find a clock.

After forty hours' working ship
I've done the best I can
So I'm going to find the galley
To get a bellyful of scran.

After many months aboard this tub
There's not much left to learn
I know now that the square end
Is the way we go astern.

Now if you broke the navy law
And looked like doing time
The skipper always make it clear
Let the punishment fit the crime.

Now attach him to the yardarm
From the thumbs let him be swinging
And leave him there suspended
Until he hears the angels singing.

The lookout yelled, 'There's land ahead,'
So as a last resort
I'll clean my boots and go ashore
Then start a girl in every port.

Well, we've just about been round the world
Are coming back where we begun
It's then we'll splice the mainbrace
With several tots of rum.

Then most will swap their hammocks
For nice soft feather beds
But I have been promoted
I am the captain of the heads.

I am what is called an old salt now
My hair is white and wavy
So what better way to spend my days
Than in the good old Aussie Navy.

# The Aussie Army

I have tried for years to get a job
To earn a decent pay
But I'm always stuck here on the dole
And just live from day to day.

So I'll settle for a different life
My mates all think I'm barmy
But I'm going to get my hair cut short
And join the Aussie army.

I stood before the recruiting sarge
He said, 'Wot are you, man or mouse?'
And the way he barked it out at me
Made me feel an utter louse.

'Now stand there at attention
Don't bat a flamin' eye
Just answer all my questions
And don't tell a flamin lie.

'Wot is yer name, how old are yer?
Have you still got all yer teeth?
Can you read and write and count to ten
Have you got bunions on yer feet?

'Now you've passed the admission test
There ain't no turning back
Go over there to yonder hut
Where you'll meet the doctor hack.

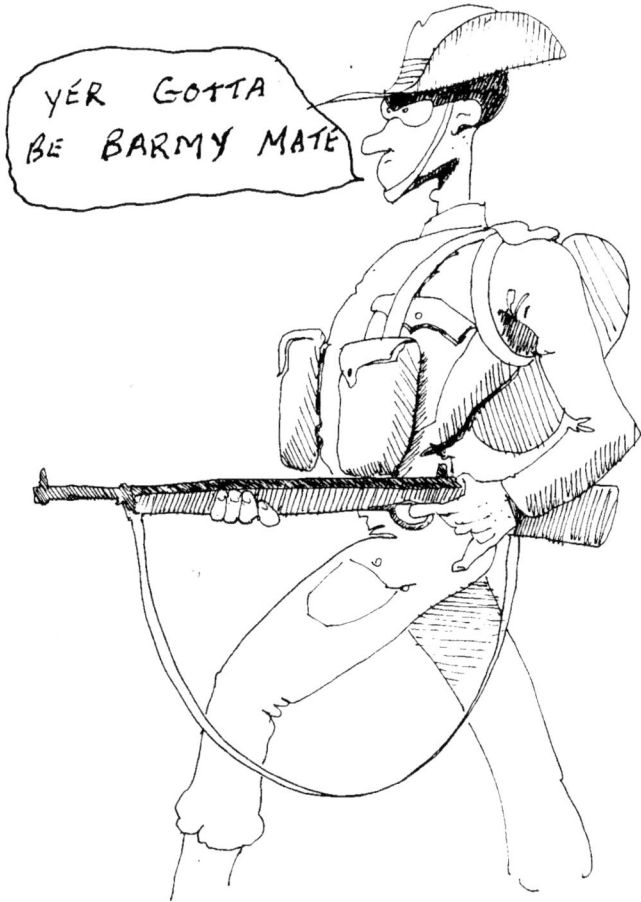

'Strip off your clothes and touch your toes
And when I poke say, "Arhhhh"
Cos when I've finished poking round
You'll wish you'd never left your Ma.

'I think you're fit enough to march
You've got two flamin' feet
You can see ahead for twenty yards
So say goodbye to civvy street.'

The bugle blew at daybreak
'Now come and enjoy the fun
You're going to run for forty k's
Before you even see the sun.

'Now get your packs up on your backs
And no backchat aimed at me
You're going to march for one hundred k's
And be back in time for tea.

I did a posting overseas
Wore my uniform with pride
And any trouble brewing
I just took it in my stride.

I've had seven years of army life
And have even learnt a trade
So when I'm back on civvy street
I've really got it made.

The time has come to say goodbye
To my mates in the Aussie Army
And now I've got a full-time job
Do you still think that I'm barmy?

# The cyclone

It's up here in Far North Queensland
Where we cannot always boast
To have a perfect weather pattern
On this most northern stretch of coast.

The weather bureau has just announced
A cyclone there might be
They have found a low depression
Away out in the Coral Sea.

We don't think much of this report
It's one that happens every year
We track them up and down the coast
But there's no cause for any fear.

Two days have passed and the bureau said
We must get through to you
Because the depression has been upgraded
To a cyclone number two.

The winds kept on increasing
A destructive force now blowing free
Because once more it's been upgraded
To a cyclone category three.

It's bearing down upon the coast
Heading towards us, so they say
As the wind gusts keep increasing
It is not a very pleasant day.

Then there comes a mighty roaring
Like a freight train passing by
As the wind gusts get much stronger
And the clouds blot out the sky.

Now the wind is really howling
A good three hundred k's or more
As the house begins to shudder
And the wind blows down the door.

The windows go, the glass blown out
The old home seems to shift
And above us there's much creaking
As the roof begins to lift.

And then there comes an eerie calm
The cyclone hasn't passed us by
It is swirling all around us
We are centred in its eye.

Then once again destructive winds
As what I built to last for years
Has begun to fall to pieces
And collapse around our ears.

The roof has gone, the walls are down
Our old home is no more
And the only things left standing
Are the stumps and half the floor.

Our ceiling fans are spinning still
Keeping up an even beat
But we won't get the breeze from them
They are halfway down the street.

The storm has passed, the calm is here
And it is now we all agree
We have total devastation
There's not a leaf on any tree.

The power has gone, the phones are out
We live in total isolation
And can only hope before too long
We have some communication.

Now it's time to think of the future
With a strong willing heart we'll endure
The discomfort of primitive living
Until we rebuild our old homestead once more.

# The Pommy—the Limey

We walked around old London town
Searching for a bed
But there was no place in this old town
Where one could lay their head.

It was a matter of survival
Only the fittest did survive
And if you pinched a loaf of bread
It was only just to keep alive.

There was no law and order
All the gentry on the take
And if they thought you misbehaved
Trumped-up charges they would make.

You would appear in the Old Bailey
Go before a magistrate
Who then would bang that gavel down
And tell you of your fate.

'I sentence you to seven years
So let's put you asunder
As I send you off in leg irons
To a place that's way Down Under.

So we became Australians
But were oft reduced to tears
For it didn't happen overnight
It took an awful lot of years.

Still the tall ships kept arriving
But they weren't having any fun
For they said, 'We've got the scurvy
And something must be done.'

Then one day a ship arrived
On board some English gannets
And in the hold for all on board
Was a load of pomegranates.

The captain said, 'A pom a day
Will help to get you through
It will beat this blasted scurvy
So they must be good for you.'

So we've had to change your title
You are no more the English Tommy
As you chew your way to better health
You have now become a pommy.

Then a captain said, 'We'll have a change
We have to keep up with the times
So we will empty out the cargo hold
And fill it full of limes.'

The limes they also did the trick
And kept the scurvy down a treat
They became a staple diet
Cos that scurvy's hard to beat.

So when you travel overseas
To that place we call Gor Blimey
You know for sure you're bound to meet
A Pommy or a Limey.

I have heard it asked so many times
How these titles got their name
So now it's down in black and white
Me thinks from whence they came.

# Proud to be Australian

Was about two hundred years ago
Since we landed on this shore
And said it's here we'll build a colony
Where white man's never been before.

We hacked down the scrub to build our towns
And they grew year by year
Then built our shops and factories
In this land we hold so dear.

We built bridges over rivers
And roads to link our towns
We put the ploughs to pastures
And turned them into rolling downs.

But soon our peace was shattered
There was the threat of war
We were needed in South Africa
To help fight against the Boer.

As yet an untried fighter
We soon became a mighty force
When we saddled up our brumbies
And became the Aussie First Light Horse.

We fought again in four more wars
Wore our battle dress with pride
We were a bit rough round the edges
But we took all in our stride.

We have battled fire and drought and flood
We have survived the great Depression
We worked this land to give us wealth
And it's been a costly lesson.

Our sporting fame is now worldwide
We keep riding on the crest
And compared to other countries
We are rated with the best.

Then when we travel overseas
All dressed in our fine regalia
As people ask, 'Where are you from?'
Then we proudly say, 'Australia.'

If I say I come from Alice Springs
You would call me a Centralian
But no matter where I come from
I'm still proud to be Australian.

# The wife

I have been a bachelor long enough
Now it's time to take a wife
To forget about my single days
And my occasional bouts of strife.

I asked her to be my partner
She knows I am true blue
So we marched up to the altar
Where I was told to say, 'I do.'

It wasn't too far down the track
I soon learned wrong from right
If I said the night was black as pitch
She would argue it was white.

If I went down to the local pub
To have a beer or two
I would come home to a frosty nest
And what should have been a stew.

If things go wrong it isn't long
She will turn up right on cue
And tell me how to fix it
Though she hasn't got a clue.

THAT'S ME OLD BATTLE AXE!

If I'm feeling rather poorly
She knows exactly what to do
'Just swallow this in one big gulp,
It must be good for you.'

She said, 'You can give up smoking,
Causes lung cancer, so they say
But I'll still have my six or eight
To see me through each day.'

Now when I go to do a job
That's when she does tempt fate
Says don't try and reach perfection
Leave it in your usual state.

She loves to tell all visitors
About all the things half done
But there's no way I can finish them
She's having too much fun.

I thought she was the weaker sex
And I am here for her protection
But when she starts to come on strong
That's when I think about defection.

Now more than thirty years have passed
I think I've weathered pretty well
One thing I know, that when I go
I have already been through hell.

I would trade my home, my car, my dog
I would even trade my life
But one thing I could never trade
Is my ever-loving wife.

# A tribute to the Vietnam Veterans

## Townsville reunion

It was in the nineteen-sixties
Into National Service you did go
To join up with the regulars
And become part of a mighty show.

The government said, 'We will pay you well
You will live off us for free
We will train you all and make you fit
It's just one big jamboree.

'We will even send you overseas
That should fill you full of cheer
Now just sign this scrap of paper
And you've just become a volunteer.

'We will ensure you won't be lonely
When you arrive in Vietnam
We will arrange a welcoming party
By the troops from Uncle Sam.'

They fought many bloody battles
And they stood there to a man
While heavily outnumbered
At the battle of Long Tan.

They took in all their worldly goods
To the Fire Support Base Coral
Then made another base camp
At a place they called Balmoral.

Their problem was the Viet Cong
Who just roamed fancy free
They would be with them for breakfast
And join the enemy for tea.

It took them all their fighting skills
Against a well trained Vietnamese
And took many years of battle
To bring the north down to its knees.

Now they leave a lot of mates behind
Who did not see this conflict through
As they head back home Down Under
To the land of the kangaroo.

There were no trumpet fanfares
There were no ticker tape parades
It was like they didn't have a homeland
They were the lost brigades.

They could not join the RSL
The upper brass said, 'No,
You only went to keep the peace,
So you are not welcome in our show.'

They asked the government for assistance
The pollies said, 'You've had your fill
So leave us alone to rest in peace
In our bunker on the hill.'

They fought years for recognition
Have broken through that wall of shame
And now have found the open door
To the service hall of fame.

Now we welcome you to Townsville
After twenty-five long years
There will be many smiles and handshakes
And we'll see many shed some tears.

It is fitting you should come back here
To where a battalion first began
And it is here that we salute you
All the Veterans of the Nam.

# A bit of paradise

There's a little bit of paradise
And that's no idle boast
It is our Magnetic Island
Off the Far North Queensland coast.

We were discovered many years ago
By a bloke named Jimmy Cook
Who gave our isle a mention
When he tried to write a book.

Just across the bay from Townsville
We have many holiday resorts
We are famous for our beaches
And well known for our forts.

It is a twenty-minute ferry ride
And you can bring an entourage
Or bring your car and camping gear
On the Capricornia barge.

Then hire a Moke at Picnic
To flit from bay to bay
But do not go down to Radical
You are bound to lose your way.

Then have a swim in waters blue
Skinny dippin' now there's a ban
So have your dip at Balding Bay
Where you are guaranteed a tan.

There's jet ski runs at Horseshoe
There's bears in our koala park
Or if you want to take it easy
Just row out and catch a shark.

We will let you have a game of golf
On our lovely nine-hole course
Or take a trip to Bluey's ranch
And climb up on a horse.

Of rocks there are no shortage
There's some as big as houses
We also boast we have two pubs
So we can't be classed as wowsers.

All this achieved through progress
Years of work by you and me
But let's take a trip down memory lane
And how our island used to be.

To come over from the mainland
Was a trip that took all day
To find a plot and settle down
On the beach front Horseshoe Bay.

Arcadia was the landing point
Over a very rough cut track
There to grab your stores and carry them
In a sugar bag on your back.

Hayles ferry brought us all our stores
Though they had no refrigeration
But that didn't really worry us
We were the pioneer generation.

We cooked upon an old wood stove
Our fridges ran on kerosene
The white ants ate your house and home
Then left a trail where they had been.

You had to light the Tilley lamp
Because there wasn't any power
And then sit back and wait for rain
So one could have a shower.

Then with the wet and heavy rain
Causing landslides and the muck
And washouts in the old dirt track
Where one could easily lose a truck.

We would climb the hill at Picnic Bay
Over rocks and through the scrub
Just to have a Sunday luncheon
At Harry Rowse's picnic pub.

We will keep the past around us
While those memories we retain
And hope we never have to go
Back to those good old days again.

# Growing wiser

I left off school at fourteen years
Cos there was nothing left to learn
There wasn't a thing I did not know
I was right at every turn.

Then I had to go and get a job
But found it hard to make the grade
Cos there's one thing now that I forgot
I forgot to learn a trade.

But I will be undaunted
I will live from year to year
Now I'm a man I'll start to smoke
And start drinking lager beer.

I want to buy a big fast car
Then take notice of the girls
They seem to differ from us blokes
Their hair is full of curls.

For twenty years I've plodded on
I'm mature and not so sporty
And I'll soon be on the beaten track
To where life begins at forty.

I'm on the verge of middle age
And I've woken up with a start
Instead of life beginning now
I'm starting to fall apart.

The doctor said, 'Now listen here
Take heed of what I tell
Give up the smoke, give up the grog
And you'll soon start feeling well.

'Go find yourself a steady job
That will last you all your life
Start saving up your money
Then think about a wife.'

I have kept my ear to every door
Have taken heed of what they say
And it's been to my advantage
As I live from day to day.

Now I look back on my misspent youth
For that life I do not yearn
One thing I know, the older I get
I'm never too old to learn.

# The True Blue Aussie

He was born here in Australia
And was brought up in the bush
That's where he went along to school
And learnt about the city push.

He is often over six feet tall
With looks that's hard to beat
And when he thinks of wearing boots
He's got number tens down on his feet.

He swung an axe at an early age
Cutting sleepers for the rail
And saw most of outback Queensland
While delivering the mail.

He can harness up a five-horse team
Operate a stump-jump plough
And even though before he talked
He had learnt to milk a cow.

He came through the Great Depression
When there just wasn't any work
But he soon went and found a job
Out past the back of Bourke.

He spent time up in the Territory
With no thought of turning back
As he kept Matilda Waltzing
Along a straight and dusty track.

He has swum the Murray River
Can kick a football half a mile
He will have a bet on anything
And always wears his Aussie smile.

He has even tried the boxing tent
Where you can make a buck of two
If you last three rounds with Punch Drunk Pete
Or the toff from Woolloomooloo.

He took up arms to go and fight
Wore his battle dress with pride
A bit rough round the edges
But he took all in his stride.

He's worked around the shearing sheds
Had a go at droving cattle
He's weathered fire and drought and flood
And life's been one constant battle.

He's a pretty easygoing bloke
Does not very often skite
But do not call him a bludger
Unless you want to pick a fight.

He is the backbone of this country
An Australian through and through
So if you need a dinkum mate
Pick an Aussie, he's True Blue.

# Good old days

When we think back to our childhood
Though we thought it was a pain
We had to learn our ABC
Or get landed with the cane.

If we had a penny in our pocket
Then we really walked on air
But if we had a sixpenny bit
We were a two-bob millionaire.

Our radio was a two-band set
We couldn't get short wave
If sometimes lucky we got the News
Or listened in to Dad and Dave.

You left off school to learn a trade
Was a wheelwright you would be
You would build a wagon or a dray
It was a booming industry.

We worked all day from dawn to dusk
It was a sixty-hour week
And Sunday was a day of rest
So we had a picnic at the creek.

We didn't have electric light
We lit the good old Tilley lamp
And when you went for a holiday
You pitched a tent and made a camp.

Our cooler was an ice chest
We cooked on an old wood stove
And all our proud possessions
Were one big treasure trove.

To fire the stove and for winter warmth
We bought wood by the cord
And if you owned a motor car
It was an old T model Ford.

And when you had a family night
You didn't have much choice
You danced all night to a phonograph
It was an old His Master's Voice.

The local cop he was the law
And if you didn't mend your ways
You got a swift kick in the rear
They were the good old days.

# Growing old

When you were just a youngster
And your life had just begun
Your world was just a playground
And each day was full of fun.

Then you grew into your teens
And finally had to shave
You then went out and found a job
And became just another slave.

Too soon you got to middle age
Then woke up with a start
For instead of life beginning then
That's when you start to fall apart.

When things go wrong you start to rant
You take ten paces, puff and pant
You're looking more like eighty-five
Though still feel young and full of jive.

You try at night to reminisce
On your long and fruitful life
But with memory dim you can just recall
That you've even got a wife.

Your eyes grow dim, your hearing fades
Your tonsils start a'squeaking
And every time you go to move
The old joints they start creaking.

With all these woes the prostate goes
Then you find it hard to piddle
You eat too much and laze around
And put on inches round the middle.

Your kidneys fail and you have a fit
Your liver's shot to pieces
You used to be a fresh-faced kid
Now the old hide's full of creases.

With all these ails the old ticker fails
And they give you up for dead
Then either put you out to grass
Or shoot you full of lead.

But now they fill you full of wonder drugs
And keep their fingers crossed
That you'll linger on a few more years
Before they toss you in a box.